planet EARTH

Earth's Rocks and Fossils

By Jim Pipe

Science curriculum consultant: Suzy Gazlay, M.A.,
science curriculum resource teacher

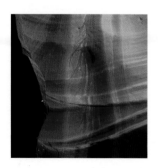   

Gareth Stevens
Publishing

Please visit our web site at www.garethstevens.com.
For a free catalog describing our list of high-quality books, call 1-800-542-2595 (USA) or 1-800-387-3178 (Canada). Our fax: 1-877-542-2596

Library of Congress Cataloging-in-Publication Data available upon request from the publisher.

ISBN-13: 978-0-8368-8918-5 (lib. bdg.)
ISBN-10: 0-8368-8918-5 (lib. bdg.)
ISBN-13: 978-0-8368-8925-3 (softcover)
ISBN-10: 0-8368-8925-8 (softcover)

This North American edition first published in 2008 by
Gareth Stevens Publishing
A Weekly Reader® Company
1 Reader's Digest Road
Pleasantville, NY 10570-7000 USA

This U.S. edition copyright © 2008 by Gareth Stevens, Inc. Original edition copyright © 2007 by ticktock Media Ltd. First published in Great Britain in 2007 by ticktock Media Ltd., Unit 2, Orchard Business Centre, North Farm Road, Tunbridge Wells, Kent, TN2 3XF United Kingdom

ticktock Project Editor: Ruth Owens
ticktock Picture Researcher: Lizzie Knowles
ticktock Project Designer: Emma Randall
With thanks to: Terry Jennings, Jean Coppendale, Suzy Gazlay, and Elizabeth Wiggans

Gareth Stevens Editor: Jessica Cohn
Gareth Stevens Creative Director: Lisa Donovan
Gareth Stevens Graphic Designer: Alex Davis

Photo credits (t = top; b = bottom; c = center; l = left; r = right):
Alamy: 15rt, 18ct. Corbis royalty free: 16lb. istock: 6lc. Layne Kennedy/Corbis: 25tl. NASA: 29rb. Natural History Museum: 22c. Photolibrary Group: cover. Rex Features: 19cb, 21 main. Shutterstock: title page all, contents page, 4lt, 4lc, 4lb, 4cb, 4–5 main, 5rt, 5rc, 5rb, 6l (top 3), 6l (diamond ring), 6 main, 7rc, 8lt, 8lb, 8–9 main, 10lt, 10–11 main, 11rt, 11rb, 12l all, 12–13 main, 13rt, 13rb, 14lt, 14–15 main, 15b, 15rc, 15rb, 17b all, 18lt, 18lc, 18lb, 18 main, 19rt, 19rc, 19rb, 20lt, 20lc, 20rt, 20rc, 21rt, 21rc, 21rb, 22b, 26b, 27 main, 28lt, 30–31 all. Science Photo Library: 7c, 7rb, 11rc, 16lc, 16 main, 23 main, 24 main, 28 main, 29 main,29rc. Superstock: 4l, 6lb, 10lb,13b, 16lt, 27rt. ticktock media archive: 7rt, 8lc, 9rt, 9rb, 13rc, 17t, 22l all, 23r all, 24lc, 24lb, 25b, 25rt, 25rc, 25rb, 26l all.

Every effort has been made to trace copyright holders, and we apologize in advance for any omissions. We would be pleased to insert the appropriate acknowledgments in any subsequent edition of this publication.

Printed in the United States of America

1 2 3 4 5 6 7 8 9 10 09 08 07

CONTENTS

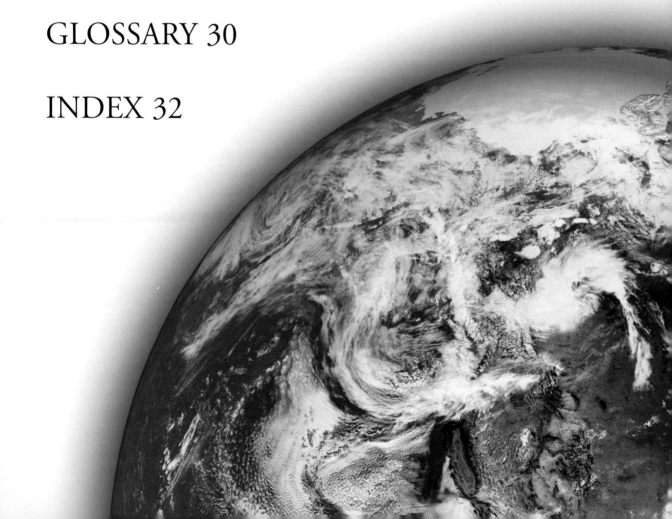

You find rocks everywhere, from mountains and riverbanks to beaches and caves.

CHAPTER 1:
Our Rocky Planet

Have you ever watched a large digging machine tear into the ground? First the machine digs through soil. If it keeps digging, it hits rock sooner or later. That's because Earth is a giant ball of rock. Layers of rock cover our planet. Earth's outer layer is called the crust.

Layers of rock are hidden under soil, water, and even ice.

Cedar Breaks National Monument is in Utah. This vast limestone cliff is shaped like a bowl. It shows the colors and layers of rock that make up Earth's crust.

While climbing a cliff face, you are actually face to face with Earth's crust.

You cannot see the rocks below our cities, but they are there!

THE HIDDEN CRUST

Water covers more than 70 percent of Earth's crust. Below the oceans, the crust is thinner than on the surface. In places, oceanic crust is only about 3 miles (4.8 kilometers) thick. The bottom of the ocean, however, is lined with mountains and valleys, just like those on land. Earth's rocky crust is also hidden under the ice at the poles.

EARTH ROCKS

Earth's crust is solid and holds land and water. On the **landmasses**, the crust is about 25 miles (40 km) thick.

The rocks are ancient in some parts of Earth's crust. Rocks have been found in Greenland that are more than 4 billion years old. Not all rock is old, however. New rocks form all the time, right below your feet!

There are three main types of rocks on Earth. They are **igneous rocks**, **sedimentary rocks**, and **metamorphic rocks**. They are all formed in different ways.

ROCK STAGES

IGNEOUS ROCKS

Igneous rocks are rocks that form from **magma** or **lava**. Magma is hot rock deep inside Earth. Lava is magma that reaches Earth's surface. Lava rises from **volcanoes**. Then it cools and hardens. **Granite** is a type of igneous rock. The giant faces of four U.S. presidents are carved in granite on Mount Rushmore in South Dakota.

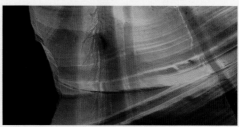

SEDIMENTARY ROCKS

Sedimentary rocks are formed from layers of tiny grains of sand and soil called **sediment**. Inside the crust, the sediment is under great pressure and heat. Over many years, the grains pack together. You can often see the layers of sediment in sedimentary rocks. **Sandstone** (above) is a type of sedimentary rock.

METAMORPHIC ROCKS

Metamorphic rocks are rocks that have changed from igneous, sedimentary, or other metamorphic rocks. This change happens deep underground. Most of these rocks form because of great heat and pressure. **Marble** (above) is a type of metamorphic rock.

GEMSTONES

Some rocks become **gemstones**. They are rough when they are first taken from the ground. But they sparkle when cut into shapes and polished. Gemstones come from minerals. Each mineral has its own shape and color.

A POLISHED SAPPHIRE

AMETHYST CRYSTALS

A RAW OPAL

A POLISHED EMERALD SET IN A RING

A POLISHED DIAMOND SET IN A RING

A RUBY AND DIAMOND PIN

WHAT ARE ROCKS MADE FROM?

Rocks are made from substances called **minerals**. These are solid chemicals found in nature. Minerals are **inorganic**. This means they do not come from plants or animals. Plants and animals need certain minerals to live, however. You need the mineral calcium for healthy bones. Another mineral is salt. Common table salt is made from the mineral halite.

WHAT ARE MINERALS?

You probably know more minerals than you think. Gold and silver are minerals. The gemstones used in jewelry are minerals. You can also find minerals in everyday objects. The graphite, or lead, in pencils is a mineral.

About 3,800 minerals have been found on Earth. Yet most are rare. Every type of rock has its own mix of minerals. For example, pure sandstone is from one mineral—quartz. Quartz is one of the most common minerals. Granite is mainly made up of three minerals. Their names are feldspar, quartz, and mica.

A mineral always has the same makeup. Each mineral has a certain shape. This piece of quartz is a mineral.

WHAT ARE CRYSTALS?

In nature, minerals usually come in shapes called **crystals**. They have a pattern of smooth faces, straight edges, and corners. Table salt crystals are shaped like tiny cubes. Zircon crystals are like pyramids. Those crystals are often used in jewelry. Most gemstones are crystals. Millions of tiny crystals often make a chunk of rock.

This is a magnified photo of the salt crystals you put on your food.

GROW YOUR OWN CRYSTALS

Materials needed
- 1/4 cup Epsom salts (from a pharmacy or supermarket)
- 1/2 cup water
- a saucepan
- a shallow bowl
- a stirring spoon
- a jar
- tissue paper
- a magnifying glass

1) Pour the water into a pan. Then add the Epsom salts. Ask an adult to heat the water. Stir until the salt dissolves. Don't let the water boil.
2) Pour half the mixture into a bowl. Pour the other half into a clean jar. Cover the jar to keep out dust.
3) After a few days, you will see small crystals in the bowl. Pour the mixture from the bowl. Dry the crystals with tissue paper.
4) Pour the fresh mixture from the jar into the bowl. Put one of the biggest crystals into the mixture.

5) After a few days, the crystal will have grown even bigger. Remove the crystal and dry it with tissue paper. Look at the crystal through a magnifying glass.

Crystals grow into weird and wonderful shapes. Some are like needles. Others look like beans or tree trunks. What shape are your crystals?

INSIDE EARTH

Temperatures increase from Earth's crust to its inner core. The inner core is nearly as hot as the surface of the Sun!

CRUST

MANTLE

OUTER CORE

INNER CORE

CHAPTER 2:
How Rocks Are Formed

More than 4 billion years ago, the Earth was a giant ball of molten, or liquid, red-hot rock. Over millions of years, the surface of the planet cooled and became the solid, rocky crust.

BENEATH THE CRUST

Under Earth's crust lies a layer of superhot rock. That layer is called the **mantle**. The mantle is solid near the top. But deeper down, it flows like melted tar. The crust floats on top of the mantle. The crust and the upper section of the mantle are known as the **lithosphere**.

The edges of Earth's tectonic plates are shown in red on this world map. The plates fit together like a jigsaw puzzle.

VOLCANOES

Volcanoes are often found along the edges of tectonic plates. They rise between two plates. Red-hot magma from deep in Earth's mantle is pushed to the surface. When magma reaches the surface it is called lava. This hot rock flows out of the volcano. The lava mixes with gas and steam. Fresh lava can be as hot as 2,200° Fahrenheit (1,200° Celsius).

EARTH'S TECTONIC PLATES

The lithosphere is broken into huge pieces. They are called **tectonic plates**. The plates support the continents and oceans. They are constantly moving, but don't worry. The movements are very, very slow. Over a long. long time, this movement creates big changes on Earth's surface.

BUILDING MOUNTAINS

When two plates move apart, hot magma can escape. It rises from the mantle and fills the gap. This makes new crust material. Iceland, in the North Atlantic Ocean, was created in this way. When two plates crash into each other, they crumple. They push giant chunks of rock upward to form mountains.

Some mountains are formed by volcanoes. The lava cools and hardens on the surface. Each time the volcano erupts, the mountain grows. Mount Fuji in Japan formed this way.

MAKING MOUNTAINS

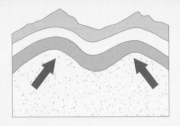

FOLD MOUNTAINS
Tectonic plate movements can force rocks to push against each other. They can fold and rise up.

The Andes Mountains
The Andes are the world's longest chain of mountains. They run down the west coast of South America. The Andes are fold mountains. They formed when an ocean plate crashed into a continental plate about 70 million years ago.

The Himalayas
The Himalayas in Asia are the highest mountains in the world. The Himalayas are also fold mountains. About 50 million years ago, a plate carrying India bumped into a plate carrying China. The plates crumpled, which pushed the rock upward.

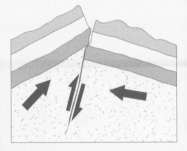

FAULT MOUNTAINS
Sometimes Earth's surface cracks. The crack is called a **fault**. Layers of rock on one side can be pushed up to form a mountain or mountain range.

Basalt is a type of igneous rock. When basalt hardens, it can form the shapes below. This is the famous Giant's Causeway in Northern Ireland.

IGNEOUS ROCKS

Besides making mountains, volcanoes help bring new rocks to Earth's surface. When hot lava comes to the surface, it cools. It forms hard igneous rocks. *Igneous* means "fiery"—just like the magma that made these rocks.

Different types of igneous rock can form. It depends on how quickly the hot rock cools. On the surface, lava cools quickly.

PLUTONS

Magma escapes through openings in Earth's crust. But the hot rock can also gather in underground ponds. Sometimes a pond of magma hardens. It then turns into a giant underground rock called a **pluton**. Some plutons are hundreds of kilometers wide. In southwest England are granite rock formations called tors (below). Tors are the remains of plutons that were once underground. The tors appeared on the surface when softer rock above them wore away.

Igneous rocks that form on the surface are called **extrusive rocks**. Basalt is a type of extrusive rock. Crystals in basalt are small because they formed quickly.

Sometimes, magma does not reach the surface. It is forced into cracks underground, where it cools slowly. It forms **intrusive rocks**, such as granite. The crystals in granite are larger because they took longer to form.

These are granite mountains in Yosemite National Park in California. These mountains were once underground magma. Over millions of years, softer rocks around them wore away.

EXAMPLES OF IGNEOUS ROCKS

PUMICE

Pumice (above) is the only rock that floats. It has air bubbles trapped inside. It can be rubbed on your hands to clean them. Tiny bits of it are in face scrubs and body scrubs.

OBSIDIAN

When hot lava flows into the sea, it cools quickly. This produces a glassy rock called obsidian. Ancient people made spear and ax heads from it. Obsidian is also shiny enough to use as a mirror.

TUFF

These statues stand guard over Easter Island, in the Pacific Ocean. The giant statues are known as moai. They were cut from volcanic rock called tuff. Some moai are nearly 15 feet (4.5 meters) tall. They weigh an average of 28,000 pounds (12,700 kilograms)!

The Rocky Mountains (above) formed about 70 million to 40 million years ago. The Appalachian Mountains (below) formed about 480 million years ago. Weathering has smoothed their shape over time.

WEATHERING

Look at the photo of the Rocky Mountains (above left). They run along the western United States and beyond. They look tall and sharp. Now look at the Appalachian Mountains (below left). They run along the eastern part of the country. They are more rounded and much lower. Over millions of years, wind, water, ice, and the Sun's heat wore them down. This is called **weathering**.

ROCKS TO BITS

Large areas of bare rock are quickest to wear away. They don't get protection from plants and soil. The rocks break down into smaller pieces, such as sand, clay, and **silt**. If you looked at sand under a microscope, you would see that it looks like the rocks that made it. They have the same minerals.

Over the last 1 million years, the Colorado River has been busy. It has been changing land around it. The river has a cut a gorge about 1 mile (nearly 2 km) deep. This gorge is the Grand Canyon!

WATER AT WORK

Waves can pound a cliff enough to make a cave. In time, the cave can become an arch (above). A caved-in arch is called a sea stack (below).

WATER POWER

Water causes weathering, too. Waves fling pebbles against cliffs. Rocks and pebbles rub against each other in rough water. This wears the rocks down into sand. Rushing water also cuts into rock. The sand and stones carried by a river also wear away at riverbanks.

BREAKING ROCKS

Mountain rocks are often shattered by ice. When water trickles into the crack in a rock, it can freeze. As it turns to ice, the water expands and makes the crack bigger. When the ice melts, more water trickles into the crack. This water will then freeze, too. Each time water in the crack freezes, the crack will get bigger. Eventually, the rock breaks along the crack.

HOW ICE BREAKS ROCKS

Materials needed
- a piece of old brick (the type used to build a house) or a piece of blackboard chalk
- a bowl of water
- a plastic bag

1) Put the brick or piece of chalk into a bowl of water. Let it soak for 4 to 5 hours.

2) Put the brick or chalk into the plastic bag. Place the bag in the freezer overnight.

3) The next morning, remove the bag from the freezer. Observe what has happened. If not much has changed, the brick or chalk has many hollows. To see a real change, you might need to leave the brick or chalk in the freezer longer.

When the water inside freezes, it swells, or expands. That breaks the brick or chalk into pieces.

SOIL

Take tiny pieces of rock. Mix them with the remains of dead plants and animals. What do you get? Soil! Different types of rocks create different soils. Plant roots speed up the process. As trees and plants grow upward, their roots grow down. Roots work into cracks in rocks. They split rocks apart. Plant activity helps break new soil into smaller pieces. Animals get in on the act, too, when they dig into the soil.

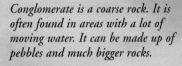

Conglomerate is a coarse rock. It is often found in areas with a lot of moving water. It can be made up of pebbles and much bigger rocks.

SEDIMENTARY ROCKS

Weathering breaks rock into small pieces. They are washed away by streams and rivers or blown by the wind. This force moving the rock fragments is called **erosion**. In time, the material lands in water. It feeds into lakes or the ocean. There, it gathers on the bottom. It sits with seashells and other minerals. This mixture of rock pieces and other material is called sediment. Over thousands of years, layers of sediment build up.

One layer of sediment is not very thick. But the layers add up. Just think of a telephone book. The thin sheets of paper add up to a heavy weight.

Layers of sediment create a heavy weight, too. They crush the layers below them. Over millions of years, the sediment turns into rocks. These are sedimentary rocks. Large sediments can create rocks called conglomerates. These rocks are made up of pebbles. They become glued together by sand that turned to stone. Medium-sized sediments create sandstone. Fine sediments turn to clay. Many familiar rocks, such as chalk, are sedimentary. **Coal** is a sedimentary rock. It formed from the remains of ancient forests.

LOOKING AT HISTORY

Sedimentary rocks have many layers. The layers formed over millions of years. They leave a record of the past. Cutting through sedimentary rock is like looking at history. You can see history that is billions of years old! Sedimentary rocks often contain **fossils**. Those are the remains of ancient living things.

These cliffs in Utah are made of sandstone. Weathering and erosion created unusual shapes. The swirling patterns in the layers of sediment were made by the wind.

SOME SEDIMENTARY ROCKS

TIGER EYE
Ironstone is a sedimentary rock. It sometimes has bands of yellow quartz. This is known as tiger eye. It is named for the yellow and brown stripes. Roman soldiers wore polished lumps of tiger eye. They believed it helped in battle.

SANDSTONE
Sandstone is used as a building material. It can be brown, yellow, red, gray, or white. Sandstone was used to build the Palace of Winds in India (above).

CLAY
Not all rocks are hard. The clay used to make pots is rock. Clay is soft enough to form with your hands. You can tell the minerals in clay from the color. Gray clay contains the mineral carbon. Red clay contains iron oxides.

STALACTITES AND STALAGMITES
Rainwater wears limestone rock away. As that water drips from the roof of a cave, some dries. It leaves behind deposits of limestone. Over hundreds of years, the limestone builds up. It forms rock "icicles." They are called stalactites. When the water hits the floor, it leaves limestone there, too. The limestone slowly builds up into columns known as stalagmites.

EXAMPLES OF METAMORPHIC ROCKS

MARBLE

Marble is a beautiful metamorphic rock. It is often used in building and sculpture. The Italian artist Michelangelo used marble for his famous statue of David (above).

GNEISS (PRONOUNCED "NICE")

Gneiss is created by heat and pressure on the igneous rock granite. The gneiss rocks above are along a river in Switzerland. They came to the surface as the Alps were formed. The rocks have been shaped by the river and weather.

TRINITITE

In July 1945, the world's first atomic bomb was tested, in a desert in New Mexico. The heat and pressure from the explosion melted the sandy ground. The sand became a shiny green rock, called trinitite.

METAMORPHIC ROCKS

Rocks form from magma, lava, and sediment. But there is yet another way that rocks are created. Metamorphic rocks can be formed from other rock. They can form from igneous, sedimentary, or other metamorphic rocks. This happens deep underground. The heat and pressure inside Earth change all forms of rock. The feel, appearance, and chemicals of the rock can be changed. It's kind of like the way a cake changes when you bake it. Rocks can also be changed when tectonic plates bump each other. The pressures and heat pound and bake the rock.

This is a slice of the rock mylonite. It is made of the minerals mica (the darker sections) and quartz (the colored sections).

HEAT AND PRESSURE

Rocks changed by heat and pressure under the ground are metamorphic rocks. *Metamorphic* means "change of form." These rocks often have swirls of color in them. This is because the rocks partly melt as they form. Some metamorphic rocks are created by heat alone. Marble is a good example. Other types, such as mylonite, are made by just pressure.

THE ROCK CYCLE

The rock cycle is always changing rocks from one type into another. It happens under our feet all the time!

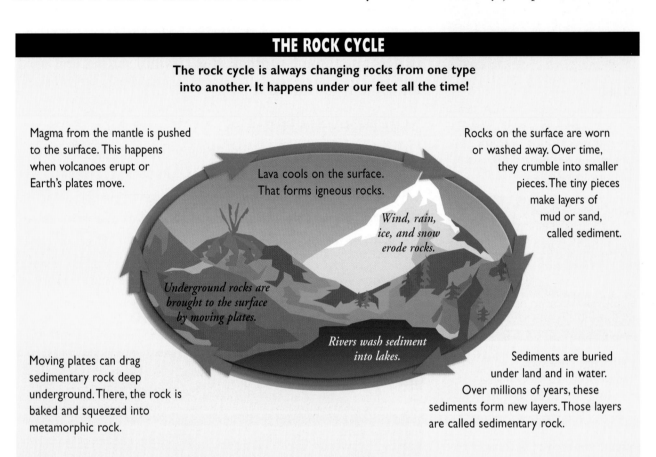

Magma from the mantle is pushed to the surface. This happens when volcanoes erupt or Earth's plates move.

Lava cools on the surface. That forms igneous rocks.

Wind, rain, ice, and snow erode rocks.

Rocks on the surface are worn or washed away. Over time, they crumble into smaller pieces. The tiny pieces make layers of mud or sand, called sediment.

Underground rocks are brought to the surface by moving plates.

Rivers wash sediment into lakes.

Moving plates can drag sedimentary rock deep underground. There, the rock is baked and squeezed into metamorphic rock.

Sediments are buried under land and in water. Over millions of years, these sediments form new layers. Those layers are called sedimentary rock.

FROM SHALE TO SCHIST

The original rock that is changed into metamorphic rock is known as parent rock. Some rocks change several times. Under low heat and pressure, the sedimentary rock shale turns into slate. When pressed and baked more, slate changes into phyllite. Finally phyllite can change into schist.

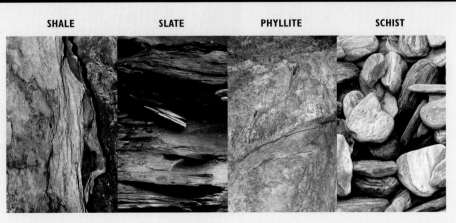

SHALE   SLATE   PHYLLITE   SCHIST

ROCK STARS

ULURU
Uluru is a huge rock in central Australia. It is one of the world's largest single pieces of rock. Uluru is 1,142 feet (348 m) high. It is a sacred site for the native Australian people.

SHIPROCK PINNACLE
The Shiprock Pinnacle is in New Mexico. It rises about 1,800 feet (550 m) above the surrounding plain. It is all that is left of an ancient volcano. It is made of hardened lava that was once deep inside Earth.

SUGAR LOAF MOUNTAIN
Sugar Loaf Mountain rises high above the city of Rio de Janeiro, Brazil. The granite peak is about 1,300 feet (395 m) high. Sugar Loaf is part of a small chain of mountains.

CHAPTER 3: ROCKS AT WORK

People have always used rocks. Common rocks, such as granite and slate, are used to build houses. Many rocks are used to make public buildings. Marble is put to work to decorate those buildings. It is cut into statues and used for columns or for tiles.

BUILDING MATERIALS

One of our most useful building materials is concrete. It is made from crushed rocks and gravel mixed with cement and sand. Cement is a mix of clay and limestone powder. Clay is also used to make bricks. The clay is baked in a large oven to make it harder and stronger.

Slate is a metamorphic rock. It can be split easily into sheets. The sheets make a good roofing material. Slate is also used to make floor tiles.

Pure sand is made almost entirely from the mineral silica. When pure sand is heated, it can be made into glass.

BLASTING OFF

Quarrying is a way to get huge blocks of rock. Workers cut rock from holes or from cliffs. This work can be hard. Often, workers blast rocks out with explosives. The explosives are also used to break rock into smaller pieces.

Powerful machines drill a line of holes in the ground at a quarry. The holes are packed with explosives. The explosives are set off from a safe distance.

PREHISTORIC USES FOR ROCK

The first mines were dug by early humans about 10,000 years ago. These prehistoric miners used small pits and tunnels to find flint. By chipping away at a rock edge, they could make flint into sharp tools and weapons. Early humans also found that when wet clay dried, it turned hard. This was how the first pottery was created. Cave paintings in France were made on rocks more than 17,000 years ago. The paints were made from crushed-up rocks and minerals.

ROCKS IN HISTORY

ROCK CITY
Petra, in Jordan, was a city cut into sandstone more than 2,000 years ago.

STONEHENGE
The famous stone circle of Stonehenge is in England. It was built in stages between 3,100 and 1,500 B.C. The posts are made from a hard sandstone.

THE TAJ MAHAL
The Taj Mahal is a famous site in India. It was built in the mid-1600s by the Emperor Shah Jahan. This wonder was built in memory of his wife. The Taj Mahal is made from marble. Marble is a favorite among artists who work with stone. The color of marble changes with the light. It has a fine grain. That can make it easier to cut than some other rocks.

Talc is a soft mineral. It is used to make powder, paint, and crayons.

Gold is used on space helmets. The gold protects the astronauts' faces against rays from the Sun.

USEFUL MINERALS

Rocks are also quarried and mined for their minerals. These minerals provide raw materials for life. Almost all the appliances in our homes use minerals.

The memory chips inside computers are made from the mineral silica. The mineral sulfur is used to make explosives. It is used in acids, dyes, matches, and more. It is in rubber and medicines. Farmers spray crops to kill bugs. The sprays have minerals in them.

If a quartz crystal is pressed hard enough, it will make an electric charge. Quartz crystals are used in clocks and watches.

Copper ore was first mined about 10,000 years ago. It was used in weapons and jewelry. Today, it is used to make wires and pipes.

IDENTIFYING MINERALS

No two minerals are the same. Every mineral has its own features. Hardness is measured on a scale devised by Friedrich Mohs. On his scale, one is the softest mineral and 10 is the hardest.

FEATURE	DIAMOND	CRYSTAL QUARTZ	GRAPHITE
CLEAVAGE How does a mineral break?	When struck, it can break in four directions	No specific way	Breaks perfectly in one direction
A STREAK What is the color if you crush it into powder?	White	White	Gray-black
HARDNESS How easily does it scratch?	10 Mohs (maximum)	7 Mohs	1–2 Mohs (1 is minimum)
LUSTER Is it shiny?	Very shiny	Glassy	Shiny when wet
TRANSPARENCY How easy is it to see through?	Transparent	Translucent	Opaque
COLOR Some minerals have several colors.	Clear	White, purple, yellow, green, and blue	Dark gray or black

Miners use a drill to remove gold from a mine in South Africa.

IMPORTANT ORES

Pure gold is mined from rocks in the ground called **ores**. Some ores have silver and iron. Others have tin and copper. The ore that contains gold is often found in hard rock. It is often deep underground. To get it, workers use drills and cutting machines. Gold can appear as a thin line running through rock. That line is called a vein. Pure gold can also appear as large lumps, called nuggets.

DIAMONDS ARE FOREVER

Diamonds are the hardest material on Earth. Drills with diamond tips are tough. They can cut through any other material. Heat and pressure deep below Earth's surface turn the element carbon into diamonds. Diamonds are brought to the surface by volcanoes.

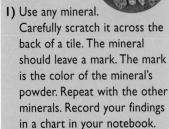

THE BIRTH OF A FOSSIL

Some ancient plants and animals ended up under sand and mud. Over many years, more mud and sand covered the remains.

The heavy layers of sand and mud above the remains put pressure on them. The remains hardened into solid rock. The bones of the animals disappeared. Minerals took the place of the bones. The rock turned into copies of the bones—fossils!

Fossils get pushed up to the surface when Earth's crust moves. They also appear after the rock wears away around them.

CHAPTER 4: FOSSILS

Many rocks under your feet are millions or even billions of years old. Looking at layers of rock, we see Earth's history. One of the best ways to study Earth's past is looking at fossils.

Fossils are the rocky remains of animals and plants that lived millions of years ago. Almost all fossils are found in sedimentary rock. This type of rock is found in swamps, lakes, and oceans. Many fossils are of animals that lived in or near water. Scientists have discovered fossils of fish. They have discovered bird, insect, and flower fossils. They have also found fossils of giant dinosaurs!

Some fossils actually power our cars. They heat our homes. Fossils from plants and tiny animals turn into **fossil fuels**. Coal, gas, and oil are all fossil fuels.

Forty dinosaur nests and eggs were found in Montana. They belonged to a plant-eating dinosaur. The fossils showed how these dinosaurs laid their eggs. They were laid in a big group, just as many birds do today. This image shows what such a nest must have looked like.

WHAT'S INSIDE?

Fossils aren't just bones. They can be the remains of plants or of animals' teeth and shells. In some cases, fossils of animals' organs have been found. In the 1990s, a dino heart fossil was found in South Dakota. Sometimes ancient insects ended up in the sticky liquid from pine trees. Over millions of years, the liquid hardened. It became the yellow gemstone amber. The insects were trapped inside.

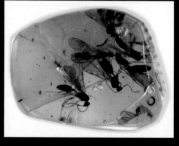

MAKING FOSSILS

Materials needed
- shells or tough leaves with big veins
- a lump of modeling clay
- a rolling pin
- cooking oil
- plaster of Paris
- water

1) Roll out the lump of clay. Make it flat and smooth. Press a shell or leaf into the clay.
2) Carefully pull the object out of the clay.

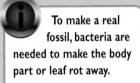 To make a real fossil, bacteria are needed to make the body part or leaf rot away.

3) Rub a small amount of cooking oil into the hole left in the clay. Then make some plaster of Paris. Mix two parts plaster with one part water.
4) Quickly spoon about 0.5 inch (1 centimeter) of plaster into the print.

In nature, minerals in underground water fill the space left by rotting bodies or leaves. This takes millions of years.

5) Leave the plaster to completely dry. Peel away the clay. You now have a cast of the original object.

 This is what happens in nature. A fossil is a cast of an animal or a plant.

This rock contains fossils of marine creatures. They lived about 440 million to 360 million years ago. They captured food using their feathery arms.

FOSSIL HISTORY

The history of Earth is broken into a series of times called eras. Each era has its own range of fossils. This time line gives us a guide for dating rocks.

PALEOZOIC ERA

BEFORE 540 MILLION YEARS AGO

Simple plants and animals appear.

540–500 MILLION YEARS AGO

The first animals with skeletons appear.

Ammonite

500–435 MILLION YEARS AGO

Primitive fish and shellfish, such as ammonites, appear.

435–410 MILLION YEARS AGO

Land creatures and the first fish with jaws appear.

Cephalaspis

410–355 MILLION YEARS AGO

Trees and insects appear. The seas are filled with bony fish, such as *Cephalaspis*.

355–295 MILLION YEARS AGO

The first forests grow.
The first reptiles appear.

295–251 MILLION YEARS AGO

Conifer trees appear. So do reptiles with long spikes on their backs.

THE TIME LINE IS CONTINUED ON PAGE 25

DINOSAUR HUNTING

Would you like to track down a dinosaur? You need to find sedimentary rock from the right period. Let's say you want to find *Tyrannosaurus rex* fossils. You need rocks that were formed about 65 million years ago. Look in areas where rocks wear away quickly. Places with rain or wind are good for fossils.

DIGGING FOSSILS

Getting fossils out of the ground is hard work. Picks can remove large chunks of rock. The last bits of rock are chipped away with small hand tools. Glue is sprayed on fossils to stop them from breaking. Then they are wrapped in layers of plaster and taken to a laboratory.

TRACE FOSSILS

Fossil hunters also look for trace fossils. These are marks made by animals. They could be footprints. They could be holes in the ground. They could be eggs or dung.

Finding fossilized tracks can tell us a lot about an animal. They can show whether an animal was part of a group. They can also show whether animal dragged its tail or even if it had a limp.

Scientists can learn a lot from dinosaur dung fossils. Some scientists spend their whole lives studying dino fossils! They can tell whether a dinosaur was a meat eater or a plant eater. They can also determine what animals a meat eater fed on.

Most work on fossils takes place in the laboratory. **Paleontologists** *are scientists who study fossils. They work with drills, picks, needles, and brushes. They use tools to chip away bits of rock around a fossil.*

WHO'S THE BIGGEST?

For many years, scientists believed *Tyrannosaurus rex* was the largest meat-eating dinosaur. Then, in the mid-1990s, *Giganotosaurus* was discovered. Scientists believe this dinosaur may have been up to 46 feet (14 m) long. In 2006, new research showed *Spinosaurus* was even bigger than *Giganotosaurus*! *Spinosaurus* was up to 49 feet (15 m) long. It had a jaw like a crocodile's.

Spinosaurus

MESOZOIC ERA

Eoraptor

251–200 MILLION YEARS AGO
One of the world's first dinosaurs, *Eoraptor*, appears. There are also mammals and plants that bear seeds.

200–145 MILLION YEARS AGO
Large and small dinosaurs appear. Flying creatures evolve.

Triceratops

145–65 MILLION YEARS AGO
Huge dinosaurs, such as *Triceratops* and *T. rex*, appear. But they die out at the end of this period.

CENOZOIC ERA

65–1.75 MILLION YEARS AGO
Giant mammals appear. So do huge hunting birds. The first relatives of humans also appear.

Smilodon

1.75 MILLION YEARS AGO TO NOW
This is the time of ice ages. There are mammals such as *Smilodon*. Modern humans, *Homo sapiens*, appear.

HOW COAL IS FORMED

SWAMP

PLANT DEBRIS

About 300 million years ago, swamps covered much of Earth. Trees and other plants around them would die. The dead plants settled to the swamp bottoms. There, this matter began to rot.

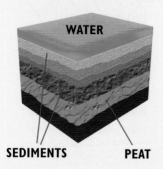

WATER

SEDIMENTS   PEAT

The rotting matter formed peat. This spongy material was buried under more layers.

COAL

Millions of years of pressure and heat turned peat into coal.

FOSSIL FUELS

The remains of plants and animals did not just become fossils. They turned into coal, oil, and natural gas, too. We call these materials fossil fuels. These materials formed more than 300 million years ago. That is before the time of the dinosaurs.

Millions of years ago, land was covered with swamps. The swamps were filled with huge trees and other large plants. They died and rotted at the bottom of water.

COAL, OIL, AND GAS

Coal looks like a hard, black rock. It is actually the remains of large swamp plants.

Oil and gas are other fossil fuels that formed with coal. Tiny marine plants and animals called plankton died and sank to the seabed. They were buried in clay and mud. Over millions of years, these sediments turned to rock. Heat and pressure underground made the plankton turn to oil and gas.

These fuels took millions of years to form. We say they are **nonrenewable resources**. Once they have been used up, they cannot be replaced.

DRILLING FOR OIL

A drill strikes oil. A thick, black liquid, called **crude oil,** pours out of the ground. The gas we put in our cars, however, is clear. That's because the oil from the ground is taken to a **refinery**. There, it is separated into different liquids. These liquids are then made into all sorts of products. Some are used to make crayons and plastics. Other are used to make jet fuel, heating oil, and even makeup for your face!

Oil is often found below the sea. That's why oil rigs are built on platforms at sea. Oil and gas get piped to shore from the rigs. Some platforms float. Others sit on legs that rest on the seabed.

Coal miners use computers to help them remove coal from below ground. The computers can control drills. This image shows a control panel used for a coal mining operation.

FROM SHELLS TO CLIFFS

The oceans absorb gases from the atmosphere. The gases include carbon dioxide. That gets turned into carbonates. Those are a mix of minerals and metals. Animals such as clams use carbonates to make their shells. When these animals die, their shells hit the seabed. Over millions of years, the shells turn into sedimentary rock. The white cliffs of Dover, in England, were made from fossils of tiny sea creatures.

READING ROCKS

Every rock tells a story. Studying fossils in rocks tells how Earth's crust moved around. For example, the fossils of sea animals were found at the top of Mount Everest, the tallest mountain in the world. This tells us that Mount Everest's rocks formed under the ocean. Fossils in rocks also tell us how plants and animals have changed. Over millions of years, they have become the wildlife we know today.

FOREVER GONE

Fossils can also tell when and how sudden changes happened. For example, what caused dinosaurs to die out? That happened around 65 million years ago. But what caused it had been a mystery.

*This art shows the Chicxulub Crater soon after its creation. That is a huge **impact crater** in Mexico. Impact craters form when space rocks hit Earth. Chicxulub is more than 100 miles (160 km) across. Many scientists believe dinosaurs died out when it hit.*

In the 1970s, scientists Luis and Walter Alvarez came up with an answer. They found a lot of one mineral in certain rocks. That mineral is called iridium. The rocks dated from the period when the dinosaurs died out. The mineral is a sign of huge volcanic blasts. It can also show that a giant space rock hit Earth. Other rocks seemed show that water and rock were thrown into the air. This suggested that Earth was hit by a giant **asteroid**. Perhaps the asteroid wiped out the dinosaurs!

CLIMATE CHANGE

Studying rocks helps scientists understand the past. It also helps them understand life today. Looking back, they see changes in weather and **climate**. Our weather is changing again. Our planet is getting warmer. Looking back may give us clues as to what will happen next.

This is the Cave of Crystals in Mexico. The cave contains some of the largest crystals in the world.

STUDYING ROCKS

GEOLOGISTS

Scientists who study rocks are called **geologists**. By looking at ancient rocks, geologists have determined that Earth is about 4.5 billion years old.

TECH TOOLS

Creep meters are buried underground. They watch the movements of Earth's plates. This helps scientists predict **earthquakes**. A creep meter can show when plates move by just a hair.

ROBOT SCIENTISTS

Sometimes volcanoes are too hot and dangerous for scientists. The robot above was used to explore a volcano in Alaska. It entered the volcano's crater. It collected gas and water samples and recorded video images.

SPACE ROCKS

Scientists want to study rocks from other planets. Mars Rover robots are studying and collecting rocks from Mars. Scientists still need to figure out how to get the rocks back to Earth!

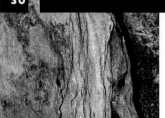

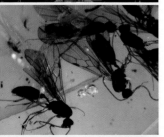

GLOSSARY

asteroid: jagged space rock that orbits the Sun. Most are found between Mars and Jupiter in an area called the asteroid belt. Some asteroids can be nearly 600 miles (1,000 km) across.

climate: the average weather in an area over a long period of time

coal: A hard, black rock-like fossil fuel. Coal is the fossilized remains of large swamp plants that lived 300 million years ago.

crude oil: the natural state of petroleum. This fossil fuel is formed from decaying plants, animals, and other organisms.

crust: the outer layer of Earth that consists of landforms and the ocean floor. The crust is about 25 miles (40 km) at its thickest point.

crystal: a solid mineral with a repeating pattern of particles. Amethysts, diamonds, and quartz are all crystals.

earthquake: a fierce shaking of the ground caused by rocks cracking and breaking deep underground

erosion: the process of material (such as rock fragments) being carried away by wind, water, or ice

extrusive rock: an igneous rock formed from lava that has erupted from volcanoes or has been forced through cracks in Earth's surface

fault: a crack in Earth's crust where huge blocks of rock slide past each other

fossil: the remains or traces of a living thing that died long ago

fossil fuels: fuels formed from the decaying remains of animals, plants, and other organisms. Oil, natural gas, and coal are fossil fuels.

gemstone: a precious rock or mineral, such as a ruby, emerald, or pearl, that is often used in jewelry

geologist: a scientist who specializes in the study of rocks

granite: an intrusive igneous rock. Many modern monuments are made of granite.

igneous rock: rock formed from magma that has reached Earth's surface and cooled

impact crater: a hole on Earth's surface that is caused by an object from space

inorganic: something that is not living, such as metal or rock

intrusive rock: an igneous rock that forms from magma that has cooled below Earth's surface

landmass: a large area of land on which we live, such as North America and Europe

lava: molten matter from a volcano or a break in Earth's surface. Before it reaches the surface, this matter is known as magma.

limestone: a sedimentary rock composed largely of the mineral calcite.

Limestone was formed from the ancient remains of sea creatures, such as shellfish.

lithosphere: the hard outer layer of Earth. The lithosphere is formed from the crust and the uppermost part of the mantle.

magma: molten rock in Earth's mantle and outer core. Magma that reaches the surface is called lava.

mantle: the thick layer of Earth that lies between the crust and core. The mantle is about 1,800 miles (2,900 km) thick.

marble: a hard metamorphic rock that can be polished. It is often used for sculpture or as a building material.

metamorphic rock: a rock that forms when heat or pressure changes an igneous or a sedimentary rock

mineral: a solid, usually inorganic (nonliving), substance that occurs naturally on Earth. Gold, copper, iron, and halite (table salt) are all minerals.

nonrenewable resource: a resources that cannot be renewed, or replaced. Fossil fuels and minerals are nonrenewable.

ore: a rock or mineral that contains metal that can be extracted (removed). Ores are mined for the metals they contain.

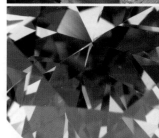

paleontologist: a scientist who studies past life on Earth, including dinosaurs

pluton: a large intrusive rock

refinery: a place where oil or metals are processed. An oil refinery turns crude oil into usable products such as fuel and plastics.

sandstone: a sedimentary rock made of mainly sand-sized grains of minerals and rocks. The grains have become naturally cemented together.

sediment: sand and soil carried by water, wind, or glaciers

sedimentary rock: rock formed from bits of soil and sand called sediment. Over time, the sediment is crushed into layers and forms new rock.

silt: tiny pieces of dirt in ponds, lakes, and rivers. Silt is a type of sediment.

tectonic plate: a giant piece of Earth's crust that floats on Earth's mantle. Plates are always moving at a very slow rate.

volcano: a hole in Earth's crust through which gas, ash, and magma escape

weathering: the breakdown of rock over a long period of time by factors such as wind and water